Acknowledgements

Thank you to Margot Northey for her persistent editing of the first edition.

Thank you to T. L Driscoll, Suzanne McGoldrick, CWO and many other military personnel for taking the time to provide their feedback. Their feedback helped make this second edition better for you.

Thank you to my graphic designers Beth for her original designs and to Isabelle Fortier for her patience and attention to detail.

Operation Who Am I®

Copyright 2020 Operation Well-Being Limited

All rights reserved.

No part of this publication may be reproduced through any mechanical, photographic, electronic or phonographic process, stored in a retrieval system or transmitted in any form, without prior written permission from the copyright owner, except in the case of brief quotations embodied in articles or reviews. Unauthorized usage is prohibited. For permission contact Operation Well-Being at info@operationwellbeing.com

Library of Congress Cataloging in Publication Data

ISBN 978-1-7777914-0-7 (hardcover)

ISBN 978-1-7777914-1-4 (paperback)

ISBN 978-1-7777914 -2-1 (electronic)

Printed in the United States and Canada

Covers designed by Getcovers.com

This book is dedicated to all serving members and Veterans.

Thank you for your courage and commitment to making the world a safer place.

WHO AM I? I moved to Petawawa to set up a clinic for veterans with mental health issues. I had set up two previous organizations that had worked with civilians with mental health issues and had completed a certificate in Meaning-Based Therapy to help me understand Viktor Frankl's philosophies.

WHY THE BOOK? One of our first clients was a man who had worked in Special Forces. He was looking for more to his life since leaving, and unfortunately, he was making dangerous choices and then wanting to end his life. He left our clinic to get more intense care, but I later learned that he had committed suicide. Before he left, he stayed around to talk to me and to others. He had attended a trauma group and was excited to be connected to other like-minded individuals. Sadly, he was not encouraged to keep trying other groups, other ways to heal. I wrote the book in hopes that I could impact more that were like this exceptional man. I carry the guilt that I could not have done more for him.

Table of Contents

Part One: Who Was I	10–93
Part Two: Who Am I Now	94–143
Part Three: Who Would I Like To Be	144–171
Developing a Personal Mission	172–179

Introduction

As a veteran, you know that a major part of your life will never be the same. Gone are the regular routines, training and military exercises that gave order and purpose to your days. For many, the years were exciting, with frequent highs: for others it was less enjoyable, but at the least, everyone learned skills, enjoyed team work and had clear responsibilities. By comparison, life beyond the military can seem isolating and lacking in purpose and identity.

However, while you are working on this program, think of it as a personal mission. For many of your group missions you have had to pack a rucksack of essentials. For this program, you will be filling your rucksack with personal essentials that reflect your own uniqueness, your own inner qualities. Everyone has them, but not everyone has discovered them.

All negative reflections or judgements that may have been drilled into your head need to be left behind because they no longer serve you. Just as you want to physically reduce the load in your rucksack and prioritize what gets packed, you also want to do the same emotionally.

Make a commitment to complete all of the questions each day, and fill your rucksack with all that you think is meaningful to you from the past and currently. By helping you discover more about your self, it will point to possibilities for a future with purpose and personal meaning.

This program is an exercise in reflection which requires you to think hard and to record truthfully what you think. Take it as seriously as you would a military exercise. Over twenty-five days you will be capturing a journal of reflections. These reflections will provide you with a greater understanding of what future choices will fit you.

Personal reflection may not come naturally to you, especially to those just transitioning from military life, where disciplined action and daily prescribed duties have been the norm. There has been little time to reflect on decisions or tasks.

But now that you are either transitioning from the military or have already left, you have time to think. Perhaps many of you wonder anxiously what the future will hold for you and how can you provide value to this new civilian environment? The skills and values that any Armed Forces member has developed are needed in the civilian world. I hope that you believe that!

This program will help you answer questions that civilians have already had to answer over the course of their career. Once you have completed the questions, you will have a greater understanding of who you are and what value you have to still contribute.

If some of these questions cause you anxiety, flashbacks and/or depression, then speak to a good friend or find a counselor (if you can) and speak to them about why this question has created some issues for you.

The Task

Each day, find a quiet spot where you can reflect for an hour without interruption. Reflect on a series of questions given for the day. Jot down your answers in this workbook, knowing that no one else will read what you write without your permission. While you may choose to answer the questions at a superficial level, you will learn more about yourself if you explain some of your answers in greater detail.

At the end of the day, we would like you to capture any reflection that had meaning. Go through our quick exercise to the left to see if the reflection can be explored a bit deeper. We have added a rucksack to the right. This is for you to capture some of your key reflections from the left side. As you did from your military exercises, fill this rucksack with all that you think is essential for your own personal mission going forward. Do not feel you have to add something to the rucksack each day, but go through the exercises to make sure. Remember you are only adding meaningful reflections to your rucksack, and only you will recognize what is meaningful to you. As you know from your own personal experiences, a lighter rucksack is also a plus. Eliminating excess baggage mentally will give you the same relief.

Halfway through the program, personal challenges are added to the program. Whether big or small, demanding or simple, all aim to expand your daily range of experience. Adding more experiences will help expedite your understanding of yourself. The experiences will also connect you to other people who may become important to you. Some may provide light relief from the demands of the exercises.

The program is divided into three sections:

1. **Who was I?**
   Your years as a child, teenager and military life.
2. **Who am I now?**
   Your life today.
3. **Who would I like to be?**

Challenge yourself to go deep, and you will reap the benefits.

Time to Start!

Who was I?
Who am I now?
Who would I like to be?

First Step: Reflect On Your Past

DAY 1

"For in every adult, there dwells the child that was and, in every child there lies the adult that will be." —John Connolly

Before you begin the daily questions, answer this question now:

What do you think you can offer to civilian life now?
We will ask you the same question at the end of this program.

Childhood

What books did you like to read? If you didn't read much, what comics or movies, video games, videos did you like?

What drew you to these favourites? Was it the characters? What did you like about the characters?

Did any character inspire you to copy him or her? Or to do something different from your regular routine? Were you inspired by the characters to do different things or to make changes in your own life?

Key reflections of yourself

1)

2)

3)

Why are these insights meaningful to you?

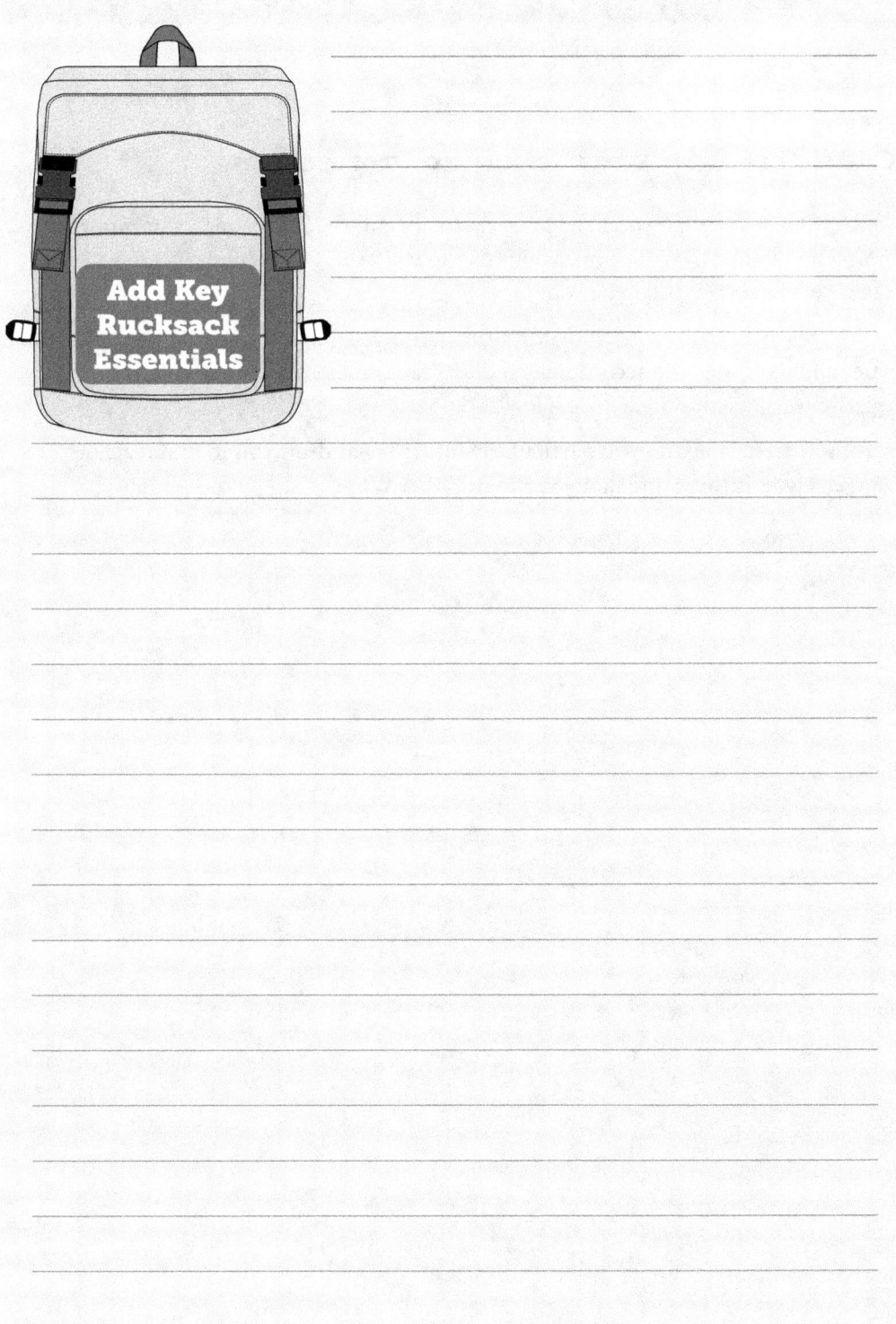

DAY 2

"Anybody who has survived his childhood has enough information about life to last him the rest of his days." — Flannery O'Connor

Understanding Your Teaching Preferences

Today's Purpose: What you liked in teachers as a child can help guide your future choices about the kinds of people you prefer to work for. For example, if you had a teacher who inspired you to be your best, what did they do?

My best teachers were those who didn't criticize or yell, but instead believed I could do better and motivated me accordingly. It didn't take much encouragement, but negative teachers intimidated me. How about you?

Was there a teacher who you particularly liked? What drew you to that teacher? Conversely, was there one that you did not like? Why?

Was there a sports coach or someone outside of school that inspired you? What did they do and how did it affect your life?

Can you remember one or two sayings that your parents taught you that hold true today? *For example, my mother never allowed me to say I was bored. She felt there was too much to do in life to be bored, and I have come to learn that she was right.*

What is your recollection of your childhood? Overall, was it mostly a good one or mostly a bad one? Explain. *Note: If you have suffered a traumatic experience in your childhood this recall effort may be difficult for you and affect you negatively. If you need support, reach out to someone you trust or consult a mental health professional.*

Key reflections of yourself

1)

2)

3)

Why are these insights meaningful to you?

DAY 3

"Teenagers complain there's nothing to do, then stay out all night doing it."
— Bob Phillips

Reflecting on Friendships and Team Dynamics

Today's Purpose: Focus on yourself and your friends. What attracted you to them? This is a time to reflect on who you were and whether you remain the same or have changed. When looking for a future career, it's crucial to find a good fit. Have you changed, or do you still have similar friends now? Would you work well with a team that has similar characteristics?

While we can't choose who we work with, we can develop a greater understanding of why we may or may not fit well with certain groups.

Secondary School Years

Who were your closest friends in high school?
What do you think drew them to you, or you to them?

**Looking back, how would you describe them now?
Would you choose them as friends today?**

How did you think of yourself during the school years? For example: nerdy, jock, weak, strong, overweight, underweight, shy, outgoing, insecure, confident?

Key reflections of yourself

1)

2)

3)

Why are these insights meaningful to you?

DAY 4

"It takes courage to grow up and become who you really are."
—E.E. Cummings

Understanding Group Dynamics from Your Teen Years

Today's Purpose: This chapter focuses on understanding groups and what drew you to certain groups as a teenager. Sometimes, looking back makes you cringe. Some people belonged to groups that bullied others, and while in the group, they didn't realize the impact they were having on outsiders. If you were outside the group, you may have wanted in, but now you look back and think it wasn't a great group.

Perhaps you still need to be part of a group because you don't feel comfortable enough to stand alone. There's no judgment here. You may prefer never to be alone and are prepared to sacrifice some of your values and needs, but consider reflecting on your non-negotiable boundaries.

In high school, was there a social group that you wanted to belong to? Why did you want to belong?

Did you feel you gave up part of who you were to be part of this group?

When you think back, did this group meet your original expectations? Explain.

Key reflections of yourself

1)

2)

3)

Why are these insights meaningful to you?

DAY 5

"It's difficult to decide whether growing pains are something teenagers have or are." —Unknown

Overcoming Academic Limitations

Today's Purpose: Too many people think they're bad at a subject simply because they didn't perform well in it. I'm thinking of math in particular. However, I believe that with good math teachers, you will succeed—but too many teachers aren't effective math instructors.

You could still become an excellent accountant, engineer, or scientist if you find the right teachers or tutors to help you understand. Think about subjects you didn't do well in. English may be another example. Consider how those early experiences may have limited your future choices.

What subjects did you like in school? Did they change over the years? If so, can you explain why?

Were you a stronger student in those same subjects you liked?

Did you excel in sports, music and/or arts? What did you like about them?

If so, are you still doing any of those same activities today?

Key reflections of yourself

1)

2)

3)

Why are these insights meaningful to you?

DAY 6

"A teenager is always too tired to hold a dishcloth, but never too tired to hold a phone." —Unknown

Positive High School Memories

Today's Purpose: Most people don't think fondly of high school, so if you can reflect on your high school years and identify a few key positive events, here's your chance to record them and carry forward those meaningful experiences.

Consider whether you're still drawn to similar events or whether you've ignored activities you used to enjoy. If so, why?

What were some especially significant events in your school years?

What made them significant?

Key reflections of yourself

1)

2)

3)

Why are these insights meaningful to you?

DAY 7

"Try to be a rainbow in someone else's cloud." —Maya Angelou

Character Development and Personal Growth

Today's Purpose: Reflect on your character at a younger age and see how much has changed. For example, if you were teased in high school, do you now stand up for others who are teased or bullied? Or do you find yourself doing the teasing without realizing you're causing harm?

Some people understand teasing dynamics if they have siblings, but many don't. Think about those earlier experiences and remember how they made you feel.

Was there a time where you stood up for someone who was being teased, or a time where you were teased?

How did you feel about people who picked on weaker or more vulnerable students?

**Were there some events where you suffered?
Or perhaps made to feel shame, guilt, humiliation?**

How did you get through those event(s)?
What coping skills did you use or do you still feel the events affecting you today?

Key reflections of yourself

1)

2)

3)

Why are these insights meaningful to you?

DAY 8

"Sometimes a person just needs a little inspiration or a different thought to get them propelled in the right direction." — Tondeleya Allen

Identifying Your Heroes and Role Models

Today's Purpose: Identify your real heroes and heroines. Our first session got you thinking about fictional characters; now consider the real people you admired and why. The characteristics of these early role models tend to stay with us throughout life, so when looking for someone to work for in your next career, you'll have a better understanding of who you'd like to work for and how they'll bring out the best in you.

For example, I was a competitive figure skater, and in my era, coaches would yell and insult. For some people, that approach worked, but for me, it didn't. I stiffened up and began to hate the sport.

Was there a high school teacher who took an interest in you?

In your high school, were there some teachers that you really liked? Why? Were there some that you disliked? Why?

Did you have any additional coaches/leaders that influenced your life in a positive way? How?

Did you have any coaches/leaders that had a negative influence on your life?

Key reflections of yourself

1)

2)

3)

Why are these insights meaningful to you?

DAY 9

Recognizing Patterns from Childhood to Teens

Today's Purpose: Discover patterns from childhood through your teenage years. Why is this important? Sometimes people discover that changing patterns later in life can indicate unaddressed early trauma. You can examine who you were and what you liked, admired, or disliked.

Trauma can significantly affect who you were and who you are now, but many people ignore these changes and assume they're fine—until they're not. However, changing patterns may also indicate growth. It all depends on what has changed and how you view your past and present.

Summary of Childhood and Teen Years

Review those two early stages in your life, and fill in the chart, transferring your essential reflections from the daily rucksacks and adding more, if necessary.

REVIEW	CHILDHOOD	TEENS
People you admired and why		
Your interests		

Summary of Childhood and Teen Years

REVIEW	CHILDHOOD	TEENS
Most significant memories		
Your personality and character		
What are you most proud of?		

Now in your reflections of your early years, did you learn anything more about yourself?

Have you noticed any patterns that you didn't recognize before?

Again, if your life has been badly affected by the experiences of trauma or abuse, consider exploring the effect further with a mental health professional.

DAY 10

"It doesn't take a hero to order men into battle. It takes a hearo to be one of those men who goes into battle." — *General Norman Schwarzkopf*

First-Year Military Experience

Today's Purpose: The first year of service often makes or breaks your military experience. If it doesn't meet your expectations, you're either disappointed and looking for an exit, or you decide to stick with it because you feel you have no other choice. Others find the military experience transformative and are excited to serve.

Each of you will have a different first-year experience. Since you're now leaving service, how did you feel during that first year? Did much change for you? Many veterans leave their next civilian career within one to two years—how can you prevent this pattern?

Your Military Years
What led you to join the military?

_____
_____
_____
_____
_____
_____
_____
_____
_____
_____
_____
_____
_____
_____

How did you feel after the first year of serving?

What regular tasks/jobs did you like best while serving?

Key reflections of yourself

1)

2)

3)

Why are these insights meaningful to you?

DAY 11

"It is foolish and wrong to mourn the men who died. Rather, we should thank God that such men lived." — George S. Patton Jr.

Career Skills and Vocational Assessment

Today's Purpose: Many of you will complete more extensive vocational exercises to answer questions like todays, so either summarize your key learnings or, for those who haven't done any assessments, answer these questions and perhaps explore additional vocational or career skills exercises.

There are many free career tools available for military personnel, so I don't want to spend excessive time in this area.

What challenges did you enjoy? Was one too much for you and why? Provide a few examples.

What tasks/jobs, experiences did you dislike?

What did others appreciate about you (personality, work ethic, skills)?

Key reflections of yourself

1)

2)

3)

Why are these insights meaningful to you?

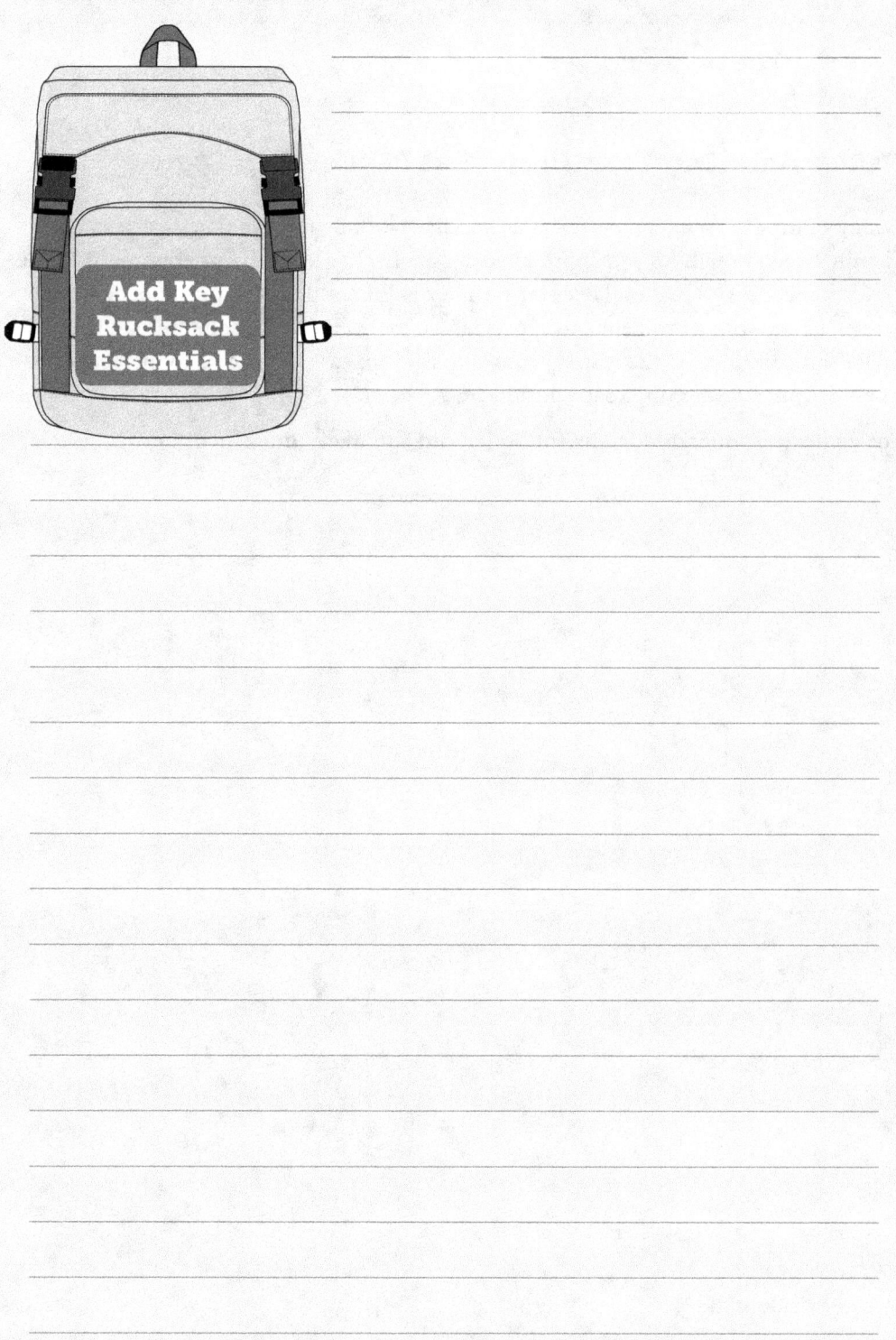

DAY 12

*"Success is not final, failure is not fatal!
It is the courage to continue that counts."* — *Winston Churchill*

Understanding Your Preferred Leadership Style

Today's Purpose: What kind of boss do you like working for? No one is perfect, but identify two key qualities you appreciated about effective leaders. For example, did you prefer someone who made all decisions while you followed orders, or someone who presented you with a problem and expected you to figure out the solution? Do you prefer someone loyal to the team or someone who appears more loyal to their superiors? These are just a few examples to consider.

For whom did you like working for? What did you like about him or her?

What do you think makes a good leader?
Did you try to copy those same qualities in your own positions?

What are you most proud of in your time in service?

- ○ Mission
- ○ Treatment of Peers
- ○ Treatment of subordinates
- ○ A particular decision or action
- ○ Other

"New York City Guard Soldiers Learn Winter Survival Skills from Canadian army [Image 2 of 3]" by DVIDSHUB is licensed with CC BY 2.0. To view a copy of this license, visit https://creativecommons.org/licenses/by/2.0/

Key reflections of yourself

1)

2)

3)

Why are these insights meaningful to you?

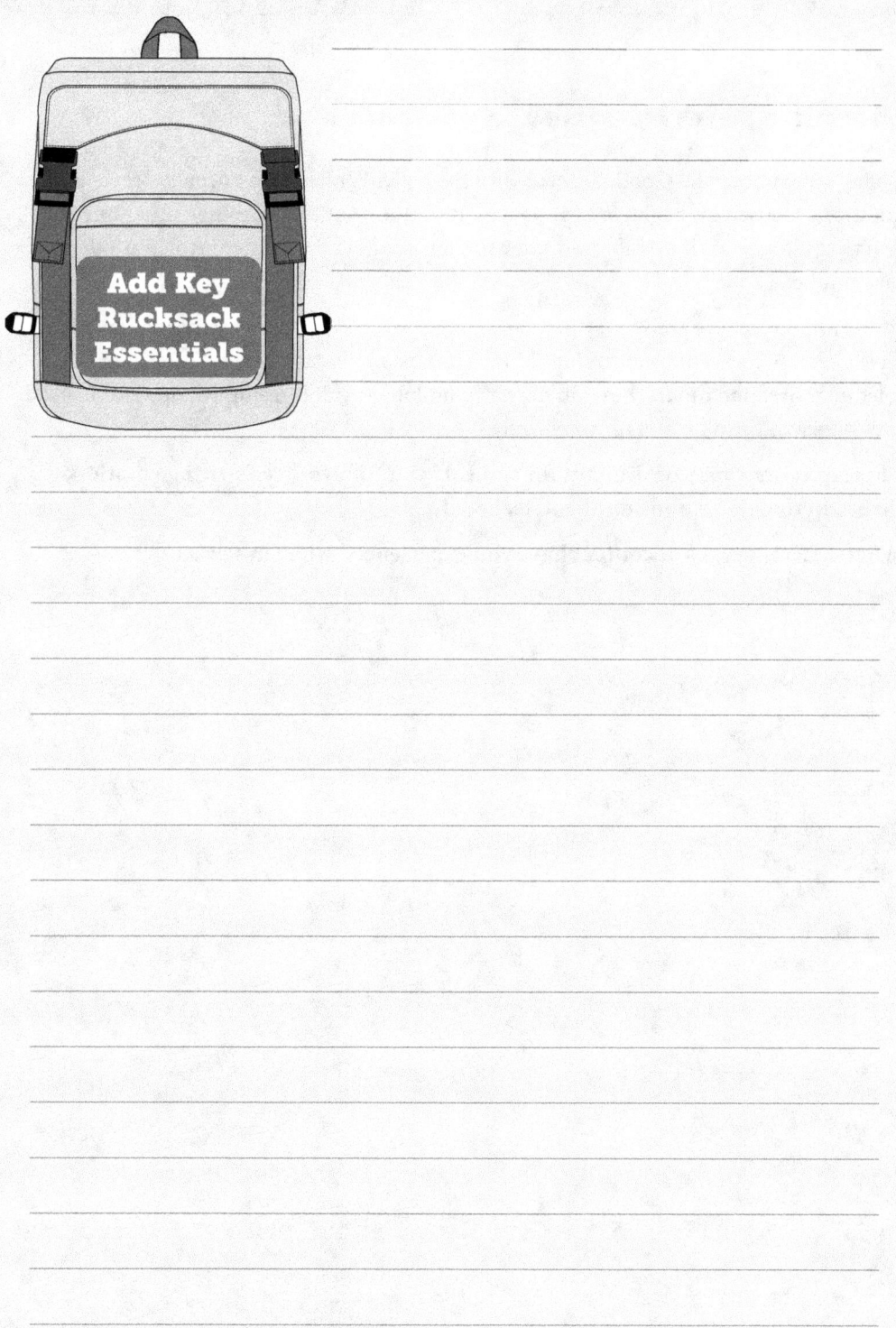

DAY 13

"True Life is lived when tiny changes occur." — Leo Tolstoy

Learning from Negative Experiences

Today's Purpose: The Good, the Bad, and the Ugly. While I don't usually create many questions focused on negative experiences, it's important to remember situations you don't want to repeat if possible. Some situations are beyond your control, but others may not be.

In the military, there aren't many situations you can control, but as a result, you may have developed exceptional coping skills that most civilians haven't. You can perhaps tolerate more than others, but you may also no longer want to simply cope and instead prefer to avoid similar situations entirely.

These questions may be difficult for some. If you find yourself getting emotional, then skip these questions until you feel ready.

What different types of conflict have you experienced while in service?

Does the experience have an impact on you today?

Was the decision or experience in or out of your realm of control?

If it was uncontrollable, have you or can you let the negative feelings go?
If you have not, then how can you help yourself to do so?
Peer support groups are often good for this if you can not get counseling.

If it was controllable by you or someone else, have you learned something from the experience to take forward?

Overall, what memories of your service "stand out" for you today?
Of course, for some of you, bad memories may stand out, but try to finish this reflection by recalling good ones as well.

Uncertain about leaving?

What would it take from the military for you to continue your service?
For example: financial support, working conditions, vocational training programs, educational opportunities.

If you feel comfortable, share your reasons... again, but with another authority figure. Who else do you know that you could approach? Nothing to lose.

Key reflections of yourself

1)

2)

3)

Why are these insights meaningful to you?

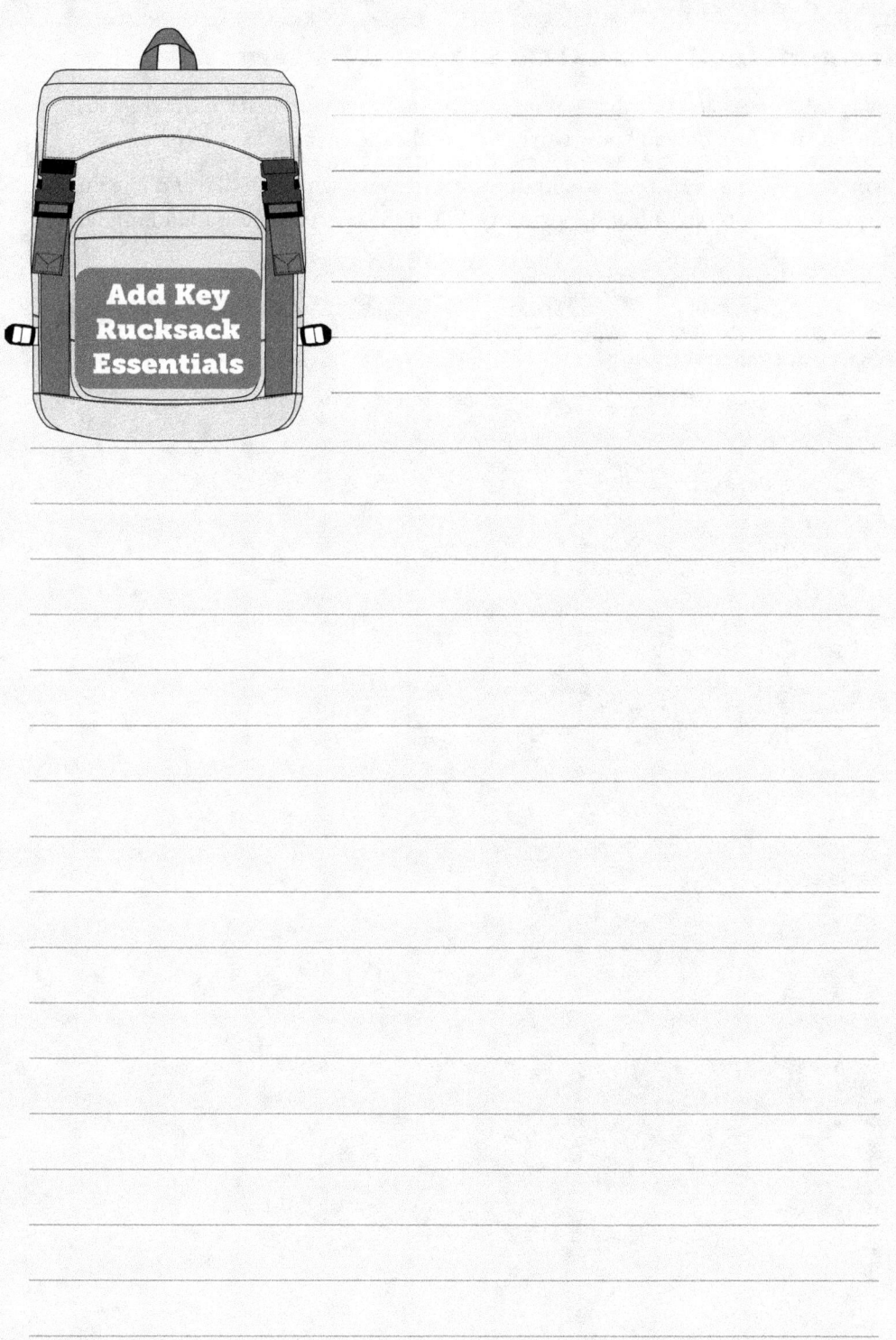

Add Key Rucksack Essentials

DAY 14
Recognizing Personal Change and Patterns

Today's Purpose: You now have more information to review patterns. Have you changed, and if so, do you know why? Do you like the changes in your patterns?

If you haven't changed, then you know going forward what you like and need in your next career or volunteer opportunity. Fill in the chart but now add in military.

Summary of Childhood, Teen and Military Life

REVIEW	CHILDHOOD
People you admired and why	
Your interests	

TEENS	MILITARY LIFE

REVIEW	CHILDHOOD
Most significant memories	
Your personality and character	
What are you most proud of?	

TEENS	MILITARY LIFE

Review

Any patterns repeating themselves from each category?

**Anything that you found surprising about yourself?
Put a star beside it. We will review this further on Day 15.**

Each day now, you will face a challenge that needs action on your part. Experience life by doing new things and pushing yourself each day. This is not about reaching a goal or measuring yourself against others, but about experiencing the process of taking a new action.

You likely won't be good at some of the activities. For others, you will decide you want to do them again! You may experience a range of emotions from frustration to silliness, but that will give you more information about yourself. Remember the expression, "You don't know what you don't know."

After each new adventure, write down what you have experienced. You may choose to accept more than one of the challenges. You may also adapt a challenge, creating one that is slightly more suitable for you. Just make sure you try to address at least one challenge each day that involves doing something new or something that you have not done for a while.

Once you have finished the challenge, check the sentence that best matches how you felt about doing it.

- ❍ Did not like this experience.
- ❍ Felt the same emotionally as when I started.
- ❍ Learned something about myself.
- ❍ Felt good and might do it again.
- ❍ Felt really good and would like to do it again.

DAY 15

"If I can not do great things, I can do small things in a great way."
— Martin Luther King Jr.

Drawing Insights from Your Patterns

Today's Purpose: Examine what insights you can draw about yourself from the patterns or breaks in patterns you've identified.

Review all of those reflections on Day 14 that you found surprising and ask yourself why they were surprising.

How have you stayed the same over the years? Are there any repeat patterns? In other words, what characteristics of your earlier years are still present within you now?

Where have you changed? Who or what influenced the change(s)?

Choose one challenge

Research and plant a new shrub or flower in your garden or buy seeds and plant one or two in a pot. Remember to water regularly.

Plan to volunteer for an organization of interest for a day or part of the day. Book a specific date.

If you cook, find and follow a new recipe for a main dish, or create a new one yourself and follow it.

Once you have finished the challenge, check the sentence that best matches how you felt about doing it.

- ○ Did not like this experience.
- ○ Felt the same emotionally as when I started.
- ○ Learned something about myself.
- ○ Felt good and might do it again.
- ○ Felt really good and would like to do it again.

Key reflections of yourself

1)

2)

3)

Why are these insights meaningful to you?

DAY 16

"I never said most of the things I said." — *Yogi Berra*

Understanding How Others See You

Today's Purpose: Focus only on the positive aspects of how others perceive you.

It's difficult to know for sure what others think of you. You may be embarrassed to ask, and your friends may be reluctant to answer truthfully. However, it's useful to reflect on the impression you leave with others through your manner, actions, or words.

This doesn't necessarily mean their impressions should determine what you do or how you think. Rather, their perceptions might enlighten you about yourself.

How would the following people describe you or likely describe you? Asking for positive feedback is usually easier for friends to give.

Family

Peers in service and/or officers

Friends

Young people: children/ nieces/nephews (this could be the most interesting)

Choose one challenge

Research a new subject online that interests you. Follow a few sites. Write down what more you could read or who you could talk with to learn more. Mark down your insights from this exercise.

Draw or paint something simple in your own living space. Use paints, colored pencils or just plain pencils. Describe your experience painting or drawing.

Listen to a new piece of music that is not from your favourite genre: such as classical, hip hop, rock or country music. How would you describe this music?

Once you have finished the challenge, check the sentence that best matches how you felt about doing it.

- ○ Did not like this experience.
- ○ Felt the same emotionally as when I started.
- ○ Learned something about myself.
- ○ Felt good and might do it again.
- ○ Felt really good and would like to do it again.

Key reflections of yourself

1)

2)

3)

Why are these insights meaningful to you?

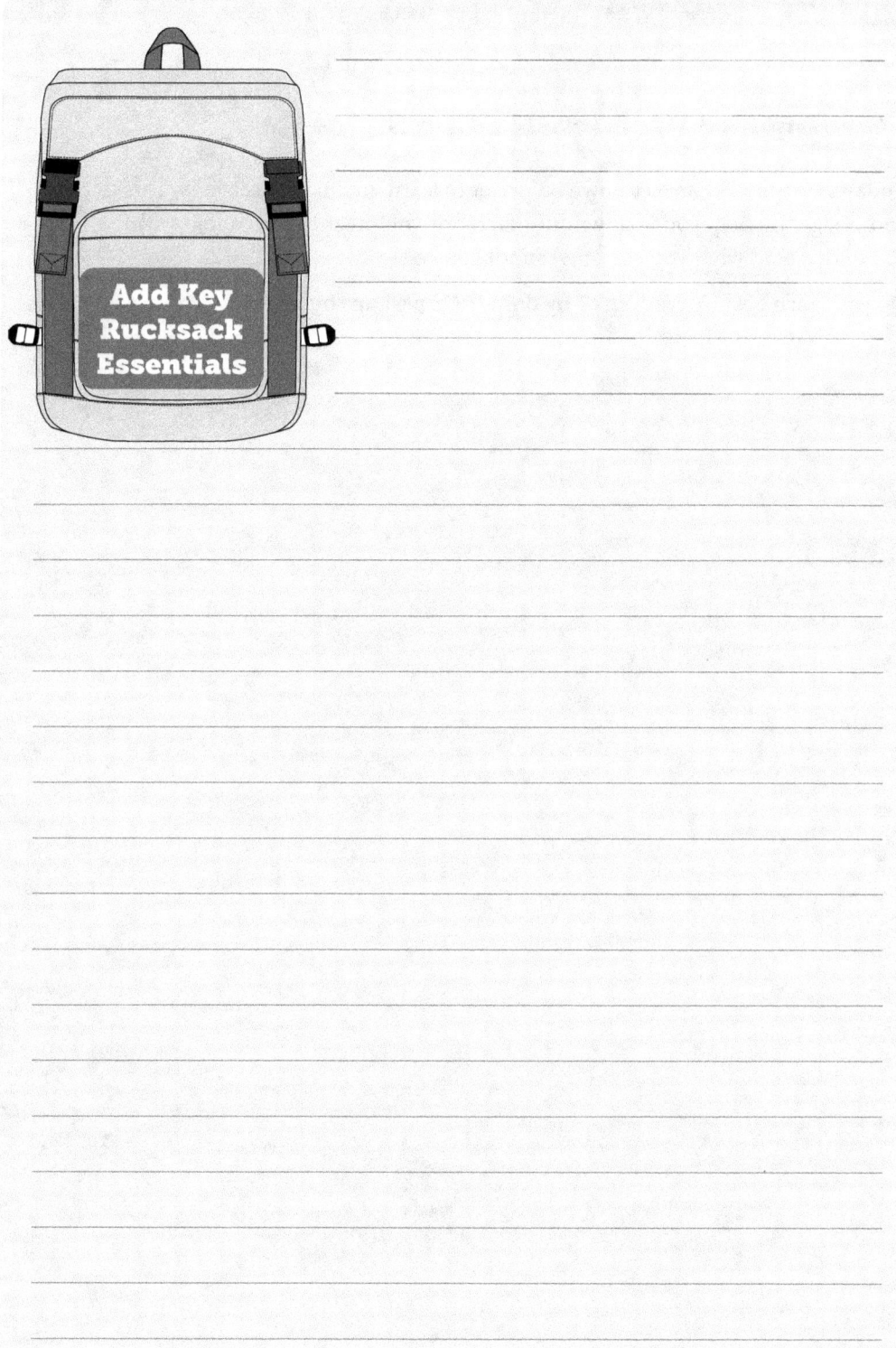

DAY 17

"A wise man changes his mind, a fool never will." — Spanish Proverb

Learning and Decision-Making Styles

Today's Purpose: Discover how you prefer to learn and make decisions. This knowledge will help you in any future career or volunteer choice, and it will also help you understand what you can and cannot control.

Do you learn best by reading or by doing? Or perhaps by both?

Do you like to learn by yourself or as part of a group?

Do you prefer to receive clear orders or to give them? Why? Perhaps, you may choose a bit of both.

In Day 13, you may have described a time when you were given directions you did not think were right. Did you have a chance to express your views or were you expected to follow orders without question? In such a circumstance today, would you prefer to remain quiet or to speak out?

How much do you think that fate or freedom determines life? In other words, is life mainly chosen for you, or do you make your own choices and create your own future?

Choose one challenge

If you have young children (nieces or nephews, neighbours), think about a humorous comment or decision one of them has made and write it down (the children will further enjoy those comments when they are older).

Go to your favourite coffee place and choose something completely different from your routine coffee/tea, something you have wanted to try. Then savour your first sip. What did you like or not like? Did it live up to your expectations?

Go to a park and walk backwards for a couple of minutes, if you can. How did you feel physically and emotionally from the experience?

Stand outdoors in a quiet area and close your eyes for a couple of minutes or longer, if you can. May need to hold a tree for balance. What do you hear? Anything that you did not expect?

Once you have finished the challenge, check the sentence that best matches how you felt about doing it.

- ○ Did not like this experience.
- ○ Felt the same emotionally as when I started.
- ○ Learned something about myself.
- ○ Felt good and might do it again.
- ○ Felt really good and would like to do it again.

Key reflections of yourself

1)

2)

3)

Why are these insights meaningful to you?

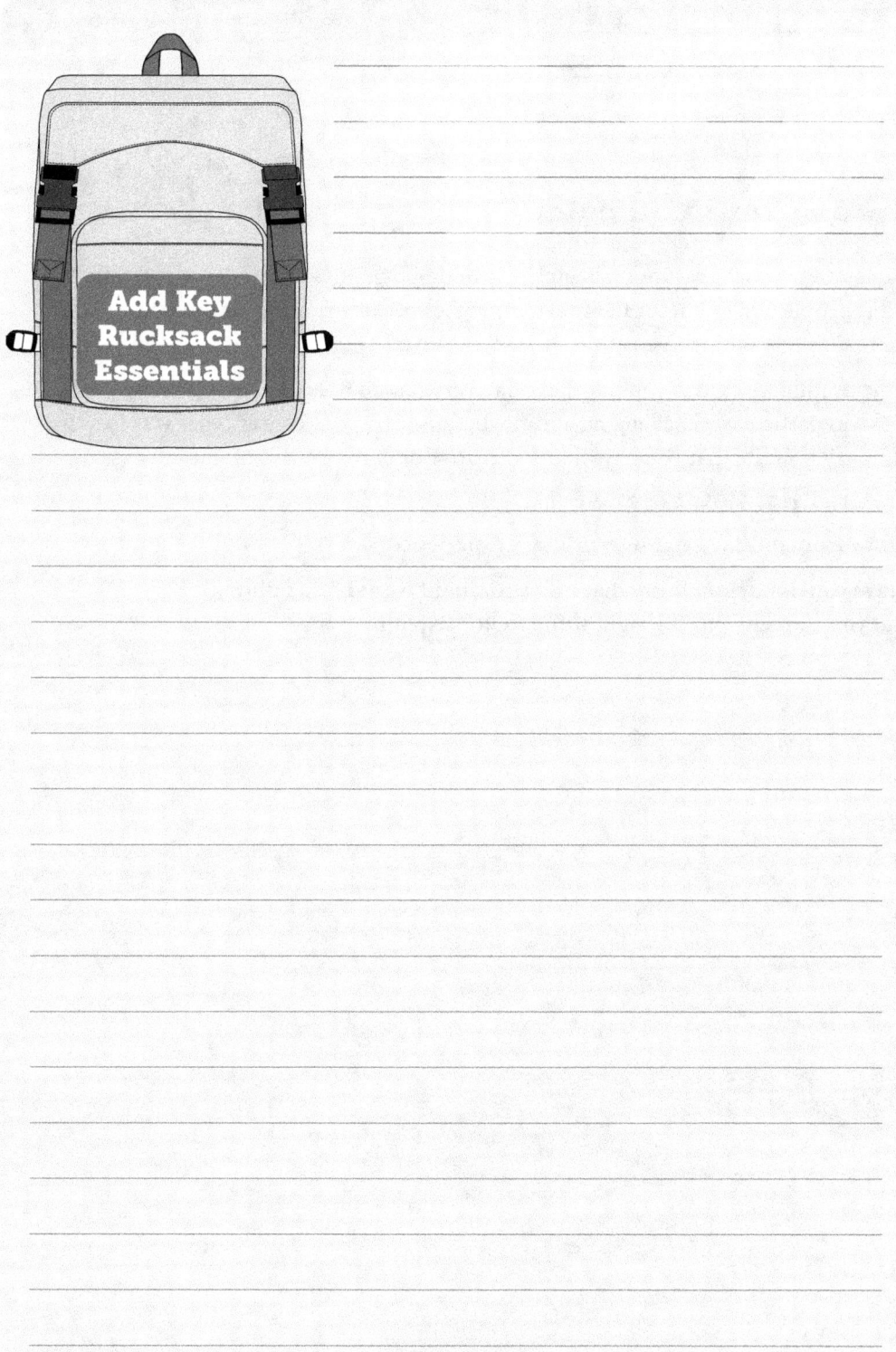

DAY 18

"As a leader you must celebrate life, you must celebrate success and paradoxically, you must celebrate heroic failures."
— Lieutenant General D.M. Mueller

Testing Your Principles

Today's Purpose: Test your principles without judgment—just observe and reflect. Most people don't fight for their own principles because doing so is difficult without sacrificing something else.

In your military career, you may have had very few choices and had to follow orders. If this was particularly challenging at times because you could see another way forward, this may indicate that you have a more creative or entrepreneurial side.

In the End, What Matters?

Draw from military and non-military experience.

Have you done something that others thought would be a failure, but you thought was the right thing to do? Explain.

Conversely, have you ever done something that you thought was right, but turned out to be a mistake? How did you respond?

Choose one challenge

Think of something that has made you smile or laugh this past week.

If there was a fire in your house, and everything burned, what would you miss most? Why is it meaningful to you?

Take a walk somewhere beautiful. Find a bench, sit down and just listen.

If you are comfortable and secure, close your eyes. What are you hearing?

If you have your eyes open, what are you seeing? Just let your mind relax and focus on the present.

Once you have finished the challenge, check the sentence that best matches how you felt about doing it.

○ Did not like this experience.
○ Felt the same emotionally as when I started.
○ Learned something about myself.
○ Felt good and might do it again.
○ Felt really good and would like to do it again.

Key reflections of yourself

1)

2)

3)

Why are these insights meaningful to you?

DAY 19

"A hero is someone who understands the responsibility that comes with his freedom." — Bob Dylan

Discovering What's Meaningful to You

Today's Purpose: When it comes to meaning, what is truly meaningful to you? Is it praise from others? Recognition for a job well done? Doing tasks that you enjoy? Trying something new and creative? Take time to identify what gives your work and life genuine meaning.

Have you ever been given credit for something that you did well, but to you, it was meaningless? How did you feel?

Can you give an example or two of something you did well after much effort, but were not given any credit or thanks for it? How did you feel? Did the experience make you reluctant to make a big effort again?

Have you taken credit for something that you had not earned, but felt it was your right to take it, or at least not to refuse it?
Has this experience affected any of your actions in the future?

Choose one challenge

Paddle, if you can, in a new place.

Take your boat to a new place to explore.

Prepare a meal for your family or a friend.

For less than $1000, visualize how you might improve the "curb appeal" of a house nearby — ie flowers, paint colours

Once you have finished the challenge, check the sentence that best matches how you felt about doing it.

- ○ Did not like this experience.
- ○ Felt the same emotionally as when I started.
- ○ Learned something about myself.
- ○ Felt good and might do it again.
- ○ Felt really good and would like to do it again.

Key reflections of yourself

1) _____

2) _____

3) _____

Why are these insights meaningful to you?

DAY 20

"Be the change you wish to see in the world." — Mahatma Gandhi

Rating Your Desire to Help Others

Today's Purpose: How highly do you rate helping others? It may seem obvious that military personnel serve to help, but for some, acts of kindness are part of their job, while for others, acts of kindness reflect who they are fundamentally. I've witnessed both types while living near the base.

As helpers know, performing kind acts makes you feel good, so when you're feeling down, try performing a small act of kindness and notice how it affects you.

Provide some examples in the past year where you have shown kindness to someone and they really appreciated it.

Family

Peers

Strangers

Do you look for opportunities to show kindness each day? Explain.

List some acts of kindness that others have done for you. Were you able to show them your appreciation at the time?

Choose one challenge

Ask someone to join in walking, paddling or biking to explore a new place. You are the organizer.

Choose a favourite exercise and find a new location or choose a different exercise at the same location.

Fish in a new location and use a different lure to catch a different fish.

Volunteer to help at your child's school for a morning or at one of their after-school activities.

Once you have finished the challenge, check the sentence that best matches how you felt about doing it.

- ○ Did not like this experience.
- ○ Felt the same emotionally as when I started.
- ○ Learned something about myself.
- ○ Felt good and might do it again.
- ○ Felt really good and would like to do it again.

Key reflections of yourself

1)

2)

3)

Why are these insights meaningful to you?

DAY 21

"If you want to fly, you have to give up what weighs you down."
— Roy T. Bennett

Emotions in Decision-Making

Today's Purpose: These exercises take decision-making to another level. Sometimes we make decisions that go against our principles because of another factor: emotions. You might gain insight into how much emotion influences your decisions.

As a military member, you sometimes have very little ability to make decisions, so how do you cope? Do you use humor? I've noticed that many veterans appreciate humor as a coping mechanism.

Are you able to identify times when an emotion — whatever it might be — influenced your decision-making? Consider emotions such as fear of failure and conflict, anger, approval seeking or envy.

Do the values and principles instilled throughout your military career affect the way you make decisions presently? For example, when you face setbacks do you seek new possibilities to move forward or do you abort the mission easily?

When you reflect on your past and present, are there particular memories and/or events that you would like to leave in the past? Are there other small achievements, you continue to be proud of?

How important is humour to you in your everyday life? Are there people in your life that share a similar sense of humour? Have you ever done something outlandish?

Choose one challenge

Don't be surprised if you begin to laugh.

| Put on some music and dance...yes, let yourself go. | Find a few good jokes online or in a book and tell them to someone. |

Once you have finished the challenge, check the sentence that best matches how you felt about doing it.

- ○ Did not like this experience.
- ○ Felt the same emotionally as when I started.
- ○ Learned something about myself.
- ○ Felt good and might do it again.
- ○ Felt really good and would like to do it again.

Key reflections of yourself

1)

2)

3)

Why are these insights meaningful to you?

Your Future

Who would
I like to be?

Who am
I now?

Who was I?

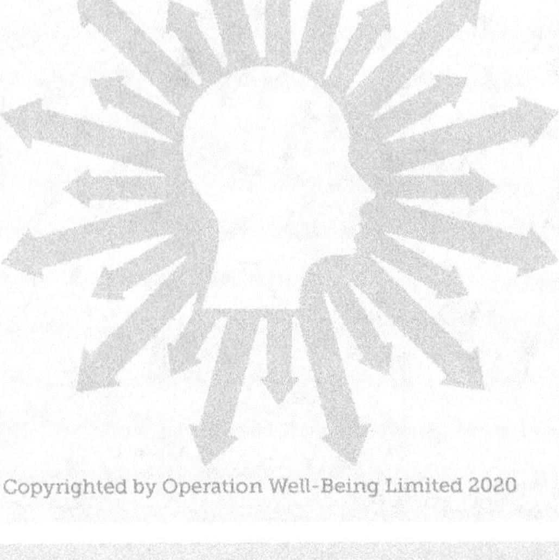

The last two sections have been a wide-ranging look backward from early years to the present. You have addressed the question *who am I* from a range of angles.

Now you can move forward, to options facing you today as a civilian.

Copyrighted by Operation Well-Being Limited 2020

DAY 22

"There are far better things ahead than any we leave behind." — C.S. Lewis

Permission to Dream

Today's Purpose: Take time to dream about what you would truly like. Now that you know more about yourself, you can address any barriers to achieving your goals with practical reasoning or recognize if they're purely emotional.

If barriers are simply emotional—such as fear—use your buddies, friends, and family to help you work through the fear and determine whether it's justified.

What more would you like to learn now, in your current circumstances?

What are your possibilities for learning it? What are the restrictions you face in doing so, and how could you overcome them?

Are there any actions you should take, so that when you are old and less physically capable, you can feel satisfied that you *lived your life to the fullest?*

What inspires you today?

Choose one challenge

Visit an elderly relative or a neighbour and spend some time talking together.

Call up someone you have not spoken to for a while. Do not text or email. Just ask them questions and listen. Do not talk about yourself for about five minutes.

Take a few of your old mugs or use a few takeout paper cups and plant some seeds of your favourite herbs using potted soil. Watch them grow.

Once you have finished the challenge, check the sentence that best matches how you felt about doing it.

- ○ Did not like this experience.
- ○ Felt the same emotionally as when I started.
- ○ Learned something about myself.
- ○ Felt good and might do it again.
- ○ Felt really good and would like to do it again.

Key reflections of yourself

1)

2)

3)

Why are these insights meaningful to you?

DAY 23

"Courage is the power to let go of the familiar." — Raymond Lindquist

Designing Your Ideal Day

Today's Purpose: Go deeper in discovering what would make an ideal day for you now. What are the barriers preventing this ideal day? Yesterday's exercises may not have unlocked all your dreams, so today we're asking the question differently to see if there's more to discover within you.

Additionally, observe another veteran whom you think is doing well—perhaps they could become a mentor to you and keep you focused on achieving your dreams.

How would you like to spend your days? *What does an ideal day look like? Take some time to visualize from the start of your day to the end. You can talk about the environment you want to have, the people you want surrounding you, the types of tasks that work best for you.*

Is there another Veteran who you admire for how he or she handles civilian life? What is it you admire?

No matter the stage in life, there is always something for you, a veteran, to achieve or contribute… an action that will give you satisfaction. What gives you great satisfaction or joy today?

Choose one challenge

If you are the cook in the family, can you reorder or redesign part of your kitchen for greater efficiency?
Create a plan of action.

Design a part of your house to give you a better workspace.

Fix something that you have left aside for a while.

Once you have finished the challenge, check the sentence that best matches how you felt about doing it.

- ○ Did not like this experience.
- ○ Felt the same emotionally as when I started.
- ○ Learned something about myself.
- ○ Felt good and might do it again.
- ○ Felt really good and would like to do it again.

Key reflections of yourself

1) _____

_____

_____

2) _____

_____

_____

3) _____

_____

_____

Why are these insights meaningful to you?

_____

_____

_____

_____

_____

_____

_____

_____

DAY 24

"There is a crack in everything, that's how the light gets in." Leonard Cohen

Reconnecting with Childhood Dreams

Today's Purpose: It may seem we're repeating questions, but many people find these questions difficult to answer initially, so I'm approaching them from different angles. These final exercises are designed to help you dream and reflect now that you've learned more about yourself.

Is there something you discovered from your childhood that you'd like to implement now? For example, I loved stories about adventurous and curious girls, but I found that I wasn't showing that sense of adventure as an adult. I promptly organized cross-country drives to discover our country alone. It was terrifying at first, but I gradually grew to enjoy the adventure, and that sense of exploration has carried forward in my life.

What is preventing you from leading a fulfilling life for yourself?

If you were given a miracle overnight and told that all of your troubles were now gone, what would be different today? What would be different about your future? Is this answer different from your answer to yesterday's *ideal day*?

Choose one challenge

> Discover some meaningful quotes that will inspire you and capture the feeling you want going forward.

> Head to your local library and explore sections of the library that you normally do not visit and see if anything interests you.

Once you have finished the challenge, check the sentence that best matches how you felt about doing it.

- ○ Did not like this experience.
- ○ Felt the same emotionally as when I started.
- ○ Learned something about myself.
- ○ Felt good and might do it again.
- ○ Felt really good and would like to do it again.

Key reflections of yourself

1)

2)

3)

Why are these insights meaningful to you?

DAY 25

"Never let the future disturb you. You will meet it, if you have to, with the same weapons of reason which today arm you against the present." — Marcus Aurelius

A Philosophical Exercise

Today's Purpose: For those interested in exploring philosophy, here's your opportunity. Today is a chance to think beyond your normal scope and consider the perspective of Marcus Aurelius—one of Rome's greatest leaders. This intellectual exercise encourages you to think about human virtues.

If you find this interesting, perhaps returning to school to study human behavior or philosophy might appeal to you.

Over two centuries ago, one of the greatest Roman Emperors, Marcus Aurelius, followed the philosophy of Stoicism. The Four Pillars of this philosophy were four virtues: **Wisdom, Justice, Courage and Moderation.**

Consider these definitions:

WISDOM
Grasping the nature of the good: understanding that virtue or wisdom itself is the only true good, and living accordingly.

JUSTICE
Going beyond today's legal meaning of fairness in laws, to include the social virtues of kindness, goodwill and benevolence.

COURAGE
The state of the soul which is unmoved by fear: military confidence; knowledge of the facts of warfare; self-restraint in the soul about what is fearful and terrible; boldness in obedience to wisdom; being intrepid in the face of death.

MODERATION/TEMPERANCE
Moderation of the soul concerning the desires and pleasures that normally occur in a life; harmony and good discipline in the soul in respect of normal pleasures and pains.

If you are interested in the Stoic four virtues, read Marcus Aurelius' *Meditations*, still widely read to this day. For a full definition and discussion of each Stoic virtue, find out more online at: donaldrobertson.name/2018/01/18/what-do-the-stoic-virtues-mean

Exercises

To what extent do the four pillars reflect your values?
Give an example of an action from your past that reflects each one.

From the limited definitions of each pillar, is there another pillar you might add?

Concluding Challenges

Summarize all that you want to put in your final rucksack. Review what you kept as meaningful thoughts in your rucksacks over the days and consider what are of the most valuable thoughts for your future.

Concluding Challenges

Create a list of all of the challenges that you enjoyed and build more. These may provide you with what Viktor Frankl called, "meaningful moments" in your future.

Concluding Challenges

Finally, do you feel you have something more or different to offer to civilian life? This question was asked at the beginning. Have you more to say now?

Going Forward in Your Life

By now, you have taken the time over several weeks to reflect on your life at different stages. You have worked through a variety of challenges. If you have completed all of the exercises and challenges, well done. Some of the daily questions would have been difficult to address. Some challenges were also difficult, but many offered creative or physical relief after the hard work of reflecting and writing.

When you look back at all you have done to complete this program, you must now have evidence of a deeper understanding of yourself. This new understanding will help you to move forward and make more meaningful choices in your civilian life.

Choices For Your Future

In the circle below, add an illustration of you in the middle. Then use arrows to outline your future focuses around the circle. Focuses may include social, family, education, health, cultural, environment and volunteer opportunities. These focuses become the basis for your personal mission outlined over the next pages.

Many of you may choose to search for paid work. While not a vocational exercise, *Operation Who Am I* has given you a good start by helping you define your strengths, desired work environment, and tasks you would like to explore.

Some of you may not be able to work full-time or even part-time, but you would like to volunteer and do something for others. See what challenges interested you and then start exploring what opportunities there are in those areas to either do as a volunteer or as a hobby. There are many non-profit organizations that would value your contributions. Start small and see how it goes. Select an organization whose actions and goals you value.

Some of you may choose to get further education. Many new opportunities exist to get training or a degree online. Some top universities, such like MIT and Harvard, offer free online courses. From the exercises in this book, see what interested you and then see if there are any courses you could take to pursue this interest. You can choose to do credit and non-credit courses.

For a few of you, questions may have raised bad memories and affected your sleep, concentration and daily life. If this is the case, seek help. Some options:

- A psychiatrist can diagnose whether you have something serious and can provide treatment and prescribe medication.
- A psychologist can diagnose and provide therapeutic treatment.
- A psychotherapist or social worker can help work through your issues using various therapies, but they do not diagnose or prescribe medications.

For those of you who would like a framework for a personal mission, the optional task on the following page can provide a visual guide to get you there.

Whatever your choices, may they lead you to new civilian joys and personal fulfilment!

Developing a Personal Mission

From your reflections, do you have any thoughts as to what your own personal mission might be going forward?

Look at the topics below and create some goals. For those that do not interest you, eliminate them. We have provided a few base questions to get you going, but you do not have to use them.

How would you rate each topic currently? Good or Needs Improvement (NI)? If it needs improvement, then be specific on what needs improvement and how you will do it.

Social

Following are just some starter questions to help you begin your thinking. Is my social life good? Do I get out of the house to meet people at least once or twice a week? Do I enjoy meeting new people or trying new things? How many close friends do I have that I enjoy, trust and know they have my back? Would I like more?

Family

How are my relationships with the following? If not strong, how could I improve them?

YOUR GOALS

Partner or spouse

Parents/in-laws

Children

Nieces/nephews

Grandparents

Education

Would I like to upgrade my education through credit courses? Would I like to learn more with little stress by taking non-credit courses? Are there topics that I would like to learn more about, but do not have the time to attend weekly courses? What books does my local library have that might interest me?

YOUR GOALS

Work/Volunteer Work

Can I work full-time, part-time or just volunteer right now? Where can I take some free vocational testing (many Veteran programs offer free vocational testing) to see what further jobs might find my skills useful? What challenges interested me enough for me to volunteer or turn into a regular hobby for me?

YOUR GOALS

Cultural

Do the arts interest me? Do I like to observe or participate in them? What shows can I attend? What classes can I take either online or in person? What organizations could I join?

YOUR GOALS

Environmental

What part of the environment interests me (ie green technology, agricultural practices, land stewardship)? Do I want to implement some green practices at home? If so, what would I like to do at home: grow vegetables, herbs, flowers or fruits or start composting? Do I want to play an advocacy role and join some local environmental groups?

YOUR GOALS

Physical

Am I interested in being in better shape? If so, in what areas and how will I do it? Do I want to play organized or informal sports? Do I want to try other physical activities that are less aerobic and more mindful such as yoga, pilates, tai chi, qi quong?

YOUR GOALS

Nutritional

How would I rate my daily diet? Could I improve upon it? Are there some areas of my health that are impacting my daily life? How many of them might be related to my diet? Are there some new recipes that I could try that would help me keep to my dietary regime?

YOUR GOALS

Brenda Northey, BA, MBA; certified in Logotherapy or meaning-based therapy.

Recently, on the advice of a Veteran Worker, Brenda turned her attention to Veterans. Having now worked with them for a few years, she knows that many veterans and those about to transition are searching for a new purpose in civilian life. Many are faltering. Building from her background and experience, "Operation Who Am I" is designed to help those facing a new civilian identity find both purpose and pleasure in their new lives.

For over twenty years Brenda has focused her attention on helping people in vulnerable communities move forward in their lives.

She founded a charity that helped homeless, single mothers get the varied assistance they needed to find work and support their children. Her innovative approach and good results changed the model for transition housing.

She worked with high-risk, unemployed adults with chronic mental health, providing a unique program for twelve weeks that got them working and hopeful about their lives once again.

She can be reached through her web-site: www.operationwellbeing.com.

www.ingramcontent.com/pod-product-compliance
Lightning Source LLC
Chambersburg PA
CBHW050416120526
44590CB00015B/1986

HOW GOOD ARE SCHOOL GARDENS?

HOW GOOD ARE SCHOOL GARDENS?

EXPLORING THE HOLISTIC BENEFITS OF SCHOOL GARDEN EXPERIENCES

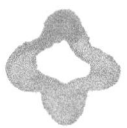

EMMA DERAINNE

Praise for *How Good are School Gardens?*

This more than just a book; it is a call to action. Emma's passionate advocacy for school gardens is contagious. *How Good are School Gardens?* is a vital resource for educators, parents and anyone interested in the intersection of education, wellbeing and the environment.

Margherita Ghezzi, Author, Program Coordinator, Education, Western Sydney University Online

How Good are School Gardens? offers a clear framework and reflections to help you set up or revive your school garden for success and sustainability. Based upon Emma's own experience and research into school gardens, this book is as practical as it informative.

Jennie Hodges, Nature-based Pediatric Occupational Therapist

Through a deep understanding of the transformative potential of school gardens, Emma Derainne illuminates how these spaces can nurture not only a connection to nature but also emotional resilience and healing. Emma's insights into the role school gardens play in fostering a sense of belonging, safety and emotional regulation are truly profound. This book is a must-read for anyone looking to create environments that support the holistic wellbeing of students.

Lisa Henderson, Teacher, School Guidance Counsellor, Trauma Researcher

How Good Are School Gardens? is a voice from teachers for teachers. The book offers practical insights into the benefits of outdoor learning for students with diverse needs. Emma beautifully captures how school gardens foster sensory engagement, social skills and emotional growth, making it a perfect tool for teachers looking to create inclusive, hands-on learning environments.

Emma A., Special Education Teacher

Published in 2024 by Amba Press, Melbourne, Australia
www.ambapress.com.au

© Emma Derainne 2024

All rights reserved. No part of this book may be reproduced or transmitted in any form or by any means, electronic or mechanical, including photocopying, recording or by any information storage and retrieval system, without prior permission in writing from the publisher.

Cover design: Tess McCabe
Internal design: Amba Press
Editor: Brooke Lyons

ISBN: 9781923215429 (pbk)
ISBN: 9781923215436 (ebk)

A catalogue record for this book is available from the National Library of Australia.

CONTENTS

About the Author		ix
Acknowledgements		xi
Introduction		1
One	Go Kick a Ball: The current state of children and nature	7
Two	Billy the Kid: Why are school gardens important?	27
Three	The Venus Flytrap: Meaning-making in the school garden	41
Four	Nurturing Resilience: Stressors and the school garden	55
Five	Guardians of Growth: The role of passionate teachers and enthusiastic supporters	67
Six	Growing Together: Peer-to-peer connection	81
Seven	Fairy Therapy: Emotional transformation in the school garden	95
Eight	Sir Worms-a-Lot: Supporting environmental sustainability	113
Nine	Roots of Connection: The holistic benefits of school gardens	131
Conclusion		149
References		159

About the Author

Emma Derainne is a teacher. With a diverse career spanning early childhood education and primary school teaching across Australia, Asia and Europe, Emma brings a wealth of experience and perspectives to her work.

Currently serving as the Program Coordinator for Early Childhood Education and Food and Nutrition Sciences at Federation University Online, Emma is dedicated to shaping the future of education through innovative curriculum development and pedagogical practices.

Emma's commitment to excellence in teaching has been recognised through various accolades, including being a finalist in the Regional Universities Network Teaching and Learning Awards in 2024. Her passion for presenting and sharing knowledge was celebrated with a People's Choice Award at the Federation University Partnership Conference in 2024 and a Dean's Award in 2020 for Leadership and Management in Education, affirming her impact and influence within the education community.

Emma is a bilingual and bicultural author. With an Associate Fellowship (Indigenous Knowledges) from the Queensland Academy of Learning and Teaching, Emma brings a culturally responsive approach to her work, ensuring that school gardens serve as inclusive, accessible and empowering spaces for all students.

Emma's academic pursuits have led her to produce a research thesis and submit journal articles as a higher degree research student of the University of Queensland – ranked number one in Australia for Food Sciences and Technologies.

Through her extensive experience, dedication to excellence and unwavering passion for education, Emma continues to place the voices of teachers, parents, students and community members at the centre of school garden research and authorship. Emma hopes that *How Good are School Gardens?* will inspire people worldwide to get involved in and harness the potential of school gardens through their multifaceted meaning as transformative learning spaces.

ACKNOWLEDGEMENTS

Firstly, I extend my deepest gratitude to my children, Arthur and Oliver. Your presence in school gardens transformed my journey as a teacher, reshaping my perceptions and experiences. Interacting with you within those green spaces influenced the meaning that I attribute to school gardens, and I am endlessly thankful for that.

To my partner, Anthony, your unwavering support sustained me throughout the writing process of this book. Thank you for the countless cups of tea and for clearing away the tea circles that amassed around my computer like a protective fort. Your patience and encouragement were invaluable.

To my parents, Frances and Stephen, thank you for instilling in me a love for nature and a deep appreciation for the simple beauty of our world. I probably could have done without the brown snake in our letterbox on the farm as I collected our post, but nonetheless, your guidance and nurturing allowed my curiosity to flourish, shaping the person I am today.

To my siblings, Luke and Courtney, thank you for being my childhood companions in mischief and adventure. Our shared experiences, from mango throwing to bull-ant races, laid the foundation for my enduring passion for nature.

To my friends, your unwavering support and encouragement sustained me through moments of doubt and exhaustion. Whether through late-night monologue audio message recordings or 4am nature walks to just 'be', your presence reminded me of my courage, passion and purpose.

To my mentors, I appreciate your support. Thanks also to my publishing team: Alicia, Tess and Brooke.

And finally, but certainly not least, I extend my heartfelt thanks to all the mentors, students, parents, teachers, carers and community members involved in school gardens worldwide. Your dedication to these green spaces is crucial, and your collective efforts are shaping a brighter future for generations to come. Together, we affirm the importance of school gardens and the profound impact they have on education and community. Thank you for your commitment and contributions. We are truly indebted to you all.

INTRODUCTION

My name is Emma and I'm passionate about school gardens.

I'm also passionate about teaching. Like many other educators, it's more than a job for me; it's a vocation. I believe teaching is about sharing time, knowledge and experiences with children and young people, helping them to see and understand the world in their unique ways. My 20-plus-year career in early childhood and primary education has always been driven by a deep interest in how children perceive their surroundings. I firmly believe that there is much adults can learn from young people's perspectives and experiences.

In my current role as a program coordinator I focus on integrating holistic learning approaches such as school gardens into the curriculum. Over the years I have developed and implemented various educational programs that emphasise experiential learning, sustainability and community engagement. I get so much satisfaction from sharing my knowledge and enthusiasm with other educators, guiding them to incorporate school gardens into their teaching practices to enhance students' health, learning and wellbeing.

The topic of school gardens became significant to me when I met a student named Billy.

I was teaching in a classroom of five- to six-year-olds when I asked, 'Where do tomatoes come from?' Billy raised his hand and proudly voiced, 'From the supermarket!' At first, I thought Billy might be trying to make his classmates laugh (he had a tendency to do this – which was both endearing and annoying). But, worse, I then realised that Billy was deadly serious. He didn't know that tomatoes grew from the soil. I looked around the classroom and there were many other blank faces. No-one knew. I was shocked. Flabbergasted. And sure, this was an inner-city school, where most of the children lived in apartments, many without even a balcony to bask in the joy of a few potted plants. But in that moment, I felt very alone, very guilty and very responsible. We had failed Billy. More importantly, despite all my good intentions and pro-environmentalist behaviours, *I* had failed Billy.

It was a call to action. Billy needed me. *All* the Billys needed me.

I realised that, in our modern society, children are increasingly disconnected from nature. Technology has been invited into our homes, with children spending more time on 'devices' than any other generation. We live in more urbanised environments and have more structured lifestyles. We want to give our children the 'best' opportunities – to play the cello, take high-diving lessons and excel academically. So, we run our children around to various extracurricular activities with the goal of fulfilling them culturally, physically and intellectually. Through this blur, we have become used to the detachment from nature, and from each other.

This realisation prompted me to start researching school gardens. I soon found myself on a journey of discovery where I learned how crucial gardens are in schools. They offer myriad diverse benefits that go far beyond nutritional advantages. School gardens create dynamic learning environments that extend beyond traditional classroom settings, providing students with hands-on experiences in sustainability, biodiversity and environmental stewardship. School gardens can serve as therapeutic spaces, offering sensory fulfilment, promoting physical activity and supporting students to develop practical skills. Involving students in a school garden helps them understand the origins of their food, and fosters a sense of responsibility towards nature.

The therapeutic and sensory benefits of school gardens can be especially beneficial for students with special needs. The tactile engagement with plants and soil can be incredibly soothing and grounding. School gardens also promote physical activity. Engaging in gardening requires physical effort, such as digging, planting and weeding, which helps to improve students' overall fitness and health.

School gardens also play a significant role in developing practical skills. They teach valuable life skills, from growing and harvesting plants to understanding seasonal cycles and ecological relationships. These skills contribute to greater self-sufficiency and a deeper appreciation for nature, equipping students with knowledge and abilities that can be applied in various aspects of their lives. Additionally, school gardens enhance emotional and social wellbeing. They encourage peer-to-peer connections and improve student-teacher relationships. By providing a safe and secure environment for students to explore, learn and interact, school gardens foster a sense of community and belonging. These connections and relationships are vital for students' overall development and wellbeing.

The educational outcomes of integrating garden activities into the curriculum are substantial. Gardens serve as living laboratories where subjects such as science, maths and art come to life through real-world applications. This hands-on approach can deepen students' understanding and retention of academic concepts, making learning more engaging and effective. For instance, students might learn about plant biology by observing and tending to plants in the garden, or they might understand mathematical concepts through measuring and planning garden plots. These practical applications of academic subjects can make learning more relevant and exciting for students.

School gardens also promote community engagement. They can become hubs for community involvement, bringing together students, teachers, parents and local residents. This collective effort not only enhances the garden's success but also strengthens community bonds and encourages a shared investment in educational outcomes. Community members can contribute their knowledge, skills and resources to support the garden, creating a sense of ownership and pride. This engagement can also provide students with opportunities to learn from different perspectives and experiences, enriching their educational journey. This is particularly important for communities with a rich agricultural or cultural heritage, with skills that can be passed from generation to generation.

This book offers encouragement and support to integrate school gardening into your educational practice. These spaces support students' holistic development. By creating interactive and inclusive learning experiences, school gardens cater to diverse student needs and promote a well-rounded educational approach. The impact of these gardens extends far beyond the nutritional benefits of the produce they yield. They contribute to student growth, development and wellbeing in a multifaceted way, encompassing therapeutic, physical, practical, emotional, social and academic dimensions.

By fostering a deeper connection to nature and providing a hands-on learning environment, school gardens offer students opportunities to develop important life skills, build meaningful relationships and engage with their communities. They help students understand the broader ecological and social systems they are a part of, instilling a sense of responsibility and stewardship. In this way, school gardens not only enhance educational outcomes but also contribute to the development of well-rounded, conscientious individuals who are prepared to make positive contributions to their communities and the world at large.

This book provides practical guidance, real-life examples and reflective prompts that will help you integrate school gardening into your teaching practice. It emphasises the importance of understanding the sociocultural context of your school and tailoring garden programs to meet specific needs. The book offers strategies for community engagement, tips for maintaining safety and security, and ideas for cross-curricular learning. It encourages you to celebrate your successes, seek support when needed, and continuously adapt your approach to make the most of your school garden.

To get the most from this book, I encourage you to adopt a reflective and open-minded approach. The book is structured to guide you through various aspects of establishing and maintaining a school garden, from initial planning to integrating garden activities into the curriculum. Each chapter includes journal prompts designed to encourage reflection and planning. I suggest you keep a dedicated journal to work through these prompts, record your thoughts and develop actionable plans.

I hope you will approach this book with curiosity, flexibility and a commitment to continuous improvement. School gardens are not one-size-fits-all; they require adaptation to the unique sociocultural contexts of each school. By engaging deeply with the content, reflecting on your practices and actively seeking ways to incorporate garden-based learning, you can create enriching, sustainable and impactful educational experiences for your students.

So, let's take a walk down the garden path together. I hope, by the end of this book, you will join me in exclaiming: 'How good are school gardens?'